My Father's
Voice

My Father's
Voice

Cheryle R. Herr

Printed by Selah Publishing Group. LLC, Ariaona. The views
expressed or implied in this work do not necessarily reflect those of
Selah Publishing Group.

ISBN- 1-58930-025-4
Library Congress Catalog Card Number- 2001089212

Acknowledgements

Stephanie and Helen for the countless hours of work you put into this book. You always encouraged me to keep going. Thanks!

To many friends and family members who know me well and love me in spite of my shortcomings. You are an awesome bunch!

My husband Don, who never puts out the flame of my wild and crazy ideas. You have been the stability in my life. I love you!

Most of all I bless the Lord for speaking to me in my quiet times as well as interrupting my busy schedule to talk to me. I am nothing special in this world, but when My Father leans over and whispers in my ear, I feel like a princess. I am His beloved one. I am eternally grateful for Your love!

Introduction

As I began to work on this project, one theme seemed to come forth in all my writings. The cry of my heart was that my Father would be in complete control of all areas of my life. In 1985 the Lord called me into a special place with a special calling. He said, " Have I not commanded you? Be strong and courageous. Do not be terrified; do not be discouraged, for the Lord your God will be with you wherever you go" (Joshua 1:9 NIV).

Throughout my life, He has taken me back to that scripture to remind me it is not in my strength that I have been called, but by His strength. Every time He leads me to a new place or a new level, He takes me back to Joshua 1:9 and we start from there. He reminds me that I do not need to fear this new adventure. At those moments, He releases His grace and I walk into His arms knowing everything will fall into place.

God has called us to trust Him in all things. "Trust in the Lord with all your heart and lean not on your own understanding" (Proverbs 3:5 NIV). The Lord said, "the challenges, struggles and trials we are now facing are to lead us into the deeper walk we desire.

"I am granting you your hearts' desire, but it can only come through these challenges. You may not see the purpose now, but you will in some future day and time. The purpose is to bring you closer and into a deeper walk with your Father and to trust Him in all things."

On July 5, 1987 the Lord spoke to me in a new way that I had never heard before. I had been calling out for a deeper relationship. I knew there was more and I wanted to experience it. The Lord said, "Do not compromise. Do not look to the left or the right, but keep your eyes on me. I will prepare the way for you to go. I love you. I proved that by allowing my Son to die on the cross for your sins. Come, follow me." Ever since that day He and I have been in a relationship that I would trade for no one or no thing.

As I sat in this quiet place waiting on the voice of my Father, I began to reflect on His faithfulness to me. He has always been on time in all things. As I sat alone, I felt His presence entering the doorway. As I looked up and saw His face, there was a smile that compares to none. He loves me. He adores me. He wants to sit and chat with me. He is not only my Savior, but He is also my eternal friend. A friend like none other! He is patient, kind, loving, caring, merciful, and full of grace for me. I know all this with just a smile from Him. He hasn't even spoken yet.

He embraces me, kisses my cheek and says, "let's talk." I know that in the next few days, weeks, months, and years — as we write this book together — we will become even closer than we have ever been. My friend's name is Jesus. He is the King of Kings and the Lord of Lords. He is the kindest, gentlest person I will ever meet.

As I walked through the past 30 years, I was not aware that I was being prepared for a time such as this. I am not saying that I have arrived, but I know that my past has prepared me for the purpose of God to be fulfilled. Things have unfolded before my eyes. I know that my Father is calling me to share with you the thoughts that He has shared with me. I pray that they will bless you and minister to you as much as they have to me and those around me.

My Father's Voice

The Lord says, "I have heard your cries and I have seen your tears. I know the needs you came here with today. Allow me to minister to you. Whatever you need, accept it from me. If you want joy and peace, then take it. If you want healing, then take that also. I have come today to meet your needs. Do not leave this place today with the needs with which you came. I love you as you love Me. I desire your love and affection as you desire Mine. I need you as you need Me. Let Me wrap my arms around you and minister to you and love you. I sit upon My throne and see your worship and your love for Me. Come enter My throne room with Me. I have not turned My face from you. You are My child and I love you. I will not turn from you, My child."

❦

"When you find yourself striving to reach your Father's throne — stop. You can be so driven to find Me that you miss Me in the process. It is the flesh that strives and works to accomplish things. Run to Me, I have drawn you close. I speak to the prodigal son and daughter; don't feel unworthy to come home. I run to you and throw My arms around you. I love you."

❧

As we deal with decisions that need to be made in life, the Lord says, "The desires of your heart are pure. I see that your heart is ripped in two. You are torn between two good desires. Neither is wrong, only one is better and will prevail. Allow me the liberty to surface the better desire. Do not give in to condemnation, it is not from Me. Your heart is not only broken but the added pain of being ripped and torn is upon you. There is a purpose in all this; just trust Me. Trust is what is important at this time. Trust Me and know without a doubt that I am your God and I love you. I have your best interest at heart in all of this." "Therefore, there is now no condemnation for those who are in Christ Jesus, because through Christ Jesus the law of the Spirit of life set me free from the law of sin and death" (Romans 8:1,2 NIV).

❧

When the Lord would talk to me about prosperity I always thought He was referring to money. However, there came a time when I realized He wasn't speaking of prosperity as the world does. He said, "Prosper in all things, in all areas. Do not live in poverty, destruction, death, and devastation. Stand in battle, take the land, and walk forward without looking back, for your Father is in control of all things. I wait to give good gifts to My children. Be faithful with what I have given and more will follow." Matthew 25:14-

30 came to mind as I began to ponder this word. I had been given many talents and gifts. Have I been faithful with them? Was the Lord pleased with what I have done with them?

≈

"When your circumstance or direction changes it does not mean that I am disappointed in you or that I have left you. I am taking you to a new level. It will serve My purpose, or it will not be allowed to take place."

≈

Stand in the things of God. Desire and go after those things. I have learned that when the enemy tells me I can't, I know immediately that I can. There have been times when I truly did not understand what the Lord was doing. I felt that He said, " I have heard your cries. Do not think I haven't. I know you do not understand what is taking place. That's okay — all things are not for you to understand. Do not look at your circumstances for they are not important. It is what you gain and learn from them that is important. I love you and you can trust Me. I am walking with you in this. You know this is true because I have not allowed you to fall through the cracks. I understand and know what is happening. Just trust Me and learn from these things. This is a day of new beginnings. The promises I have given to you will begin today. Watch and be aware and know I am your God and when your enemy comes in to destroy you, you must stand and fight. Stand in My authority. Stand in My Name. Be steadfast in your warfare."

❧

"When you stand in the authority I have given to you, your enemy will flee from you. Know who you are in Me. As you stand in this authority and see the outcome, more power and authority will be placed upon you. You need to get this in your heart. You will no longer be viewed or known as being small and insignificant. You will be acknowledged as one who wins the battle."

❧

"I am the God of forgiveness and I have called My people to live lives of forgiveness. Release those you hold in bondage. Release your past to be your past and not your present. I cannot stay where unforgiveness lies."

❧

My evaluation of myself is not how My Father sees me. He said, "Your ways are not my ways, your thoughts are not My thoughts. The ways you perceive things are not how I perceive them. Surrender your thoughts to Me. Give up control of things in your life. I am the Maker of all things. Release your self into My arms and let My thoughts be your thoughts and My ways be your ways."

❧

"I love you My children, I love you. I wish you could know the depth of My love for you. Your enemy tells you that you are not worthy of anything but hand-me-downs and old things. I tell you it is a day of new beginnings. In Jesus, you are worthy of new things. You will begin to receive new things. Accept these as gifts from your Father. You will receive new and mighty things. Do not settle for old things, because the Lord your God, has new and mighty things to give you. Watch for them. Wait on them for they are coming."

❧

"I know the things that cause you discouragement and disappointment. I love you and I have your best interest at heart. I go before you, behind you, and beside you. I want you to trust in these things. You have no way to control them. That is why you must trust Me and know that I am your God. I am your Father in Heaven."

❧

"The day has come to move forward. Be aware of the new things you have tasted and loved for they will become reality. They will come to be. Acknowledge them and know I am in them. Embrace them and run with them for they are the blessings of your Father. I love you very much. You have waited and persevered and now is the time of reckoning."

❧

"You are My bride. I have called each one of you as you are, with your spots and blemishes. I love you. It does not matter what you have done or what you have been in the past. It doesn't matter what the world says, it only matters what I say. I have mercy and compassion for you. Run into My arms—they are open and waiting for you. I love you and accept you the way you are."

⚘

"I am redirecting your tastes. You have felt so much condemnation from this. You were not being rebellious or ungrateful when you were not satisfied with what you have experienced in Me. I have caused you to be unsatisfied with these things. Being complacent where you are will not work for you. I will not permit this for I have greater things for you to experience. If you become satisfied with what I have done, you will not move on. As you walk these things out, I will take you to a new level, a deeper place in Me. As you long for this place, I have the freedom to move you into this place. You are not ungrateful nor do you have a rebellious spirit within you. I am moving you, prompting you and leading you into a deeper realm of who I am."

⚘

"Come My child, run, run into My arms. Lay your head against My breast and weep. Weep until there is no more within you. Release all the pain and suffering that you carry. Give it to Me. It is Mine. Release it to Me, all of it, and walk away free and at peace. I am your Father and I love you. Allow Me to hold you and to comfort you. Allow Me to take those things from you. Give me your burdens. Allow Me to carry them for you. For I am your Father, and I love you."

❧

"Trust Me in your challenges, struggles, and trials. For they will lead you into a deeper walk with Me. I am granting your heart's desire, but it can only come through these challenges. You may not see the purposes now but you will in time. The purpose is to bring us closer and into a deeper walk with each other."

❧

"Be encouraged in the silence that you feel. Do not despair in the gap you feel between us. Do not fear for I am with you in all things. Your enemy would have you believe that I have left you. Be encouraged, I stand beside you in these things. I have not left you, nor will I leave you or forsake you."

❧

"Be who I have made you. Get rid of the phony things. I do not want you to act like anything or anyone else. Get rid of the religious spirit of trying to be something you are not. Grow up and become mature. Stay on track and keep My vision at hand."

❧

"I have waited a long time for you to come to the place where you are now. I have led you here. I know the pain, frustration, anxiety and fear that you feel. I want you to be free from these things, that is why I have led you to this place. I love you, My child. I have been with you. You are not alone. I do not hate you. That is not why I have brought you through these things. I love you and want to set you free. Do not go back. It is not a mistake that you are here. I brought you here to see miracles. I did not bring you here to torture you. I love you, child. I know your disappointments. Until you deal with these things we cannot move forward. You are My child and I love you."

❧

"The only way to experience the winds is to wait on Me to lead you. You must wait on Me for everything. There is a blessing that comes with the winds."

❧

"My voice is heard in the quietness. As you steal away, run from the rat race, and sit quietly before Me, you will hear My voice. You will receive what you have come after."

❧

"My child when you come to Me in worship with an open heart as you have done today, you cause My heart to melt. You cause the tears to run down My face. When you worship like this, it causes Me to grant the desires of your heart. Know that I love you with all My heart as you love Me with all your heart."

❧

"My child won't you love Me, won't you run into My arms? I love you. I long to spend time with you. I want you to desire that within you. I want you to run into My arms and let Me hold you. Won't you bow down before Me and let Me love you and comfort you? You say you do not have time to spend with Me alone and quiet. But I have created you with a desire to want to love Me. My heart breaks and tears run down My face when you run from Me. Run into My arms and let Me hold you. How I long for this, more than you could ever desire it, I desire it."

❧

"Come to Me, to the foot of the cross. Leave your tears, struggles, problems, and heartaches there. Everything you seek and everything you desire deep within your soul is found at the foot of the cross. The peace, the love, the strength you so deeply desire is only found when you come and meet Me at the foot of the cross. Come into My arms and let Me hold you. Let Me walk with you. I have not left you nor will I leave you. I created you. I formed you."

❧

"The time has come for you to see the truth you have desired and asked to see for a long time. Open your heart, mind and soul and allow Me to flow through you. Allow Me to dwell within you. Allow Me to wrap you up and protect you. As you see the truth, there will be pain. As you seek truth, there will be struggles. But, you will know the truth and it will set you free. There is freedom in truth."

❧

"My child, I have come to you today to let you know that victory is yours. No matter what trial, hardship, battle or war you felt you faced alone — you haven't. Today, victory is yours. Embrace it and grab hold of it. Bring it unto yourself, for today victory is yours. I have come to you today, specifically to tell you that victory is yours. Do not accept the lies and deceit of your enemy. No longer believe what you have been told by him, for the opposite is true. Grab hold of this truth — of this victory. It is yours today."

❧

"My child, I have something to tell you. I have direction to give to you. I have correction, rebuke and guidance to pass along to you. I need you to sit and listen — to spend time, without a time limit. Just sit and listen to what I have to share with you. I want you to know the plans I have for you. Draw away to a quiet place and listen intently to what I have to say."

❧

The Lord showed me a vision. He holds His hands over a bucket to catch our tears as they fall. I also saw His face and as we cry, tears come down His face. As He caught each tear, He counted them. Not one went unnoticed or uncounted. He longs for us to run into His arms.

❧

"My children, My purpose for coming long ago is still the same today. I have come to give grace to those who have none, to give freedom to those in bondage, and to heal those who are ill. Know that I have come because I love you. Come and run into My arms. Ask whatever it is you need of Me today."

❧

"Child, I am more concerned about You, as My child, than I am about your title in this world. You try to obtain My love by who you are and your performance. Your obedience is what is important, not your status in this world. Let Me embrace you and hold you tight. Sit on My lap and let Me hold you tight for a long time. Do not perform any longer. Just lay and rest in My arms. Just rest in My arms."

❧

"Today, children, I must warn you to guard yourselves from lust for the things you run after and the things you embrace. Be careful of the path you place your feet upon. For your enemy brings things to you to destroy you and to cause destruction. Be careful children. Watch carefully what you seek after. Seek after Me, seek My face, allow Me to place you on the right path. Seek after these gifts, for truly you have desires in your heart for them, not because they are glorified or because someone else has them. I say to you, watch out and be cautious about what it is you desire. Do not let your enemy deceive you. Seek after Me and I will set you on your path."

❧

"Your only purpose in this life is to share My love. Let everything else go; nothing else matters. First of all, you are My child. Whatever position you hold is secondary. Your only purpose in life is to share My love. Watch your reactions to those around you and to the things of this world. Your enemy loves to push your buttons. Some things you fall into are not My will for your life. You choose those things by embracing the lust and temptations of your enemy. Watch your anger, your reactions and your responses."

❧

"I want you to come and worship Me. Your worship is a sweet aroma to My nostrils. I love your worship and I accept it. If you will worship Me and seek My face, the desires of your heart will be given. Instead of running from Me, run to Me. I want to set you free from the hindrances in life."

❧

"I will bring blessings. This means many blessings. If you expect one blessing you have already received what you expected. But if you expect much, you will receive much."

❧

"You have many reasons to have hope. I must warn you to guard yourself from looking at situations as they appear. For I tell you as quickly as these have come, they will fade away. So do not concentrate on your circumstances, but concentrate on Me. You will see devastation and destruction if you look only at your circumstances. Look to Me for discernment. I love you and I will keep you safe. Keep your eyes focused on Me child, only on Me and not what appears to be happening. Your enemy wants to destroy you in this, but I tell you there will be no death in it. There will be mercy, grace, love, and contentment if you will only stay focused on Me. I have never failed you. I have never let you fall and this time will be no different. I love you, My beloved."

❧

"Many things have I done and many things am I going to do. Watch, wait, listen and heed My call. My call will come as a trumpet sound. You will know it is Me, the Lord your God. Watch your step. Watch your stand for the Lord your God will shake all that is within you and around you. Stand firm."

❧

"I tell you My child to stand and take your rightful place. Seek your worth in My kingdom. Seek revelation of how your Father sees you. Stand in confidence, not arrogance. Stand with courage knowing your Father loves you. Let Me take your hand and let's walk into the throne room.

Seek My face. I want you to know My thoughts as to how valuable you are to Me. I love you."

❧

"I love you, My child. You know I have called you and I will provide for you as I always have. You are not alone so do not be afraid. You are in My arms, warm and safe. Settle in, be comforted and know I will lead you, guide you, and provide for you. Your Father loves you more than you could ever know. Rest assured you are not alone. Stay in touch and you will know where I am going and what I am doing. I love you and will guard you in all you do."

❧

One night when we were in a restaurant eating dinner, we had a waitress named Naomi. I knew God had a word for her so as I went through the day I kept praying. I went back to the same place that night to give her the word and she had called off work. This is what the Lord says to her and others like her, "The Lord has put you in a place of honor, not to be trampled under pigs feet. He has raised you up to a place of honor and you are not even aware of it. Hold your head high. He is going to do great things in your life. He is going to take you to the top, above those who have belittled and tormented you. No longer will you be tormented for the Lord your God has said 'enough.' He loves you. You are His child. He will protect you."

❧

"I hear you crying out. I want to pick you up and hold you and yet I can't because you won't let Me. You stand with clenched fists. You turn and walk away from Me still crying out. I see your dreams and visions but they are not My dreams and visions for you. I have better things for you but I cannot bring them to you because you have chosen your will over My will. I want you to release your will to Me so I can bring My blessings. You fight a battle that was never meant for you to fight. I have a completely different battle for you to fight— one which I will empower and strengthen you to fight. You lose battles because you fight battles that you were never intended to fight in the first place. Run into My arms and allow Me to wipe your tears. Fall prostrate before Me. Turn your will over to Me. Let Me pick you up and hold you. I love you child because you are Mine. I created you. I have your best interest at heart, but I need My will to be your will."

≫

"I will raise up warriors, those who will fight on the front lines and those who will be hidden away in their prayer closet. Your responsibility is to train them, to keep them secure in the word, to fill them with My love, to gird them. Get them ready for battle. Pray with them. Teach them My word for they will use it in battle. I have called you to pre- pare My warriors for battle."

≫

"Children, children, children, I see you looking to the left and to the right. You are looking for peace. You are looking for things of the world to satisfy your needs. You look for things to take away your turmoil and torment. I tell you today you can only find satisfaction when you find Me. Don't overlook Me. Look into My eyes. Come into My arms and you will find peace and rest. The One you run past is the One who has all these things you seek after. Come My children, come and sit with Me. Come and let Me hold you and take the torment from you. You want set free, then come, come into My arms and I will set you free for I am the Lord your God."

❧

"Prophecies from Me are not immediately built. They take time to come to pass, even years. I want you to know what I am doing and where you are headed so you can be faithful. Therefore, let Me do the things that need to be done."

❧

I saw a curtain, dark and dreary with bondage dripping from it. The Lord said," My child I see your face. I know you are seeking My face. All you need to do is push back the curtain. The side you stand on is holding you in bondage. There is death and destruction. But if you push back the curtain there is life, light, and freedom in Me. Take a physical step through the curtain. As you push it back, step to the other side. I am waiting on the other side; just push back the curtain. I will be there with open arms, with all the blessings you seek from Me."

❧

"As you walk out My will new things will take place. The old will be gone, for that time of your life is over. You are being called to walk a new path. Get ready. Be prepared, for it will come. You will not be surprised because I have told you ahead of time. Know it is from Me and have the freedom to walk it out. Get up. Get ready. Get dressed and prepare yourself for the new day, a new page, clean and fresh."

⤲

"My children today I want you to see My face. I want you to come so close to Me that I can kiss your face. I want to embrace you. I want to spend time with you so I can tell you the deepest thoughts I have of you. I want you to see My love, for you are My children and I am your Father. I miss you. I am a jealous God and I yearn for My time with you. Do not just leave Me standing alone, come close. Allow Me to hold you and cuddle you as you do with your children. You have made a right choice. You have done what I have asked, so as a result of your obedience you will see fruit — much fruit. Do not hold back, but go forward and see great things. See what I will bring your way for I am your Father. I am the great provider."

⤲

"If you are Mine, you will follow Me where I lead you without any questions as to why or where. You will just pick up and follow Me. You will move on in the future, for there will be new things taking place. I am setting them up for you now. Be still and patient and wait on Me. I am preparing every thing, right now, so they will fall into place at the proper time. You will see that all things will be new. Things will change drastically and quickly once they start. Do not fear them, it is just another realm into which I am taking you. Take My yoke upon you and you will see it is easy. This move will not be tough. It will not be hard because I have been preparing you for this. You will see many changes, so just flow with them. I will protect you against the evils of this day and against those who wish to slaughter you in battle. I will be your protector, your guard. I am the Great and Mighty One who sees all things and knows all things. Times for change will come rapidly as they have in the past. Know that I have ordained them and you will prosper from them. You are Mine and I will save you from the evils around you. I love you. I am your Father."

❧

"Child, why is it that you will embrace the lies of your enemy and yet when I tell you truth you can not accept it as truth? You allow so much destruction to take place in your life because of the lies you permit to take up residence within you. Seek out the truth. Do not allow the lies of your enemy to come in and take over. You know right from wrong. You want truth. I know you do because I see your heart and I also hear you whisper it to Me. Search deep within yourself for the lies that you have accepted as truth. Hand them over to Me. Give each lie to Me so that My truth can permeate deep within you. How I desire for you to be set free from the lies of your enemy. Come child, let's walk in this. Let's walk this to the end so you can become the person I truly meant for you to be. I love you. I desire this much more than you do. Come My beloved and know that I am your Father."

❧

"I am a shield for you. I am the protector of your soul. I am the great "I AM". I am your guide and leader. Do not fret and do not spend time in fear, for I have all bases covered. Just trust Me. I will tell you where to go and what to do. I love you, My sheep, I love you. I will not permit your enemy to devour you. Do not run from here to there looking for answers, for none will be found. Look in My face and seek My answers for they are only found in Me. Seek Me out in the midst of the turmoil. I will be found by you."

❧

"Be cautious. Again I say, be cautious. Do not fall into the trap of your enemy to get you off track. Things will fill your days in which I never intended for you to be involved. You will be safe if you stay close to Me, near My heart. Seek My face and you will know My heart."

❧

"Beware and watch the things around you, as they may not always be as they appear. Ask Me and I will show you the light from the dark. I will reveal to you the good from the bad. You will know My will in the midst of the confusion. My child, be still and wait on Me. Do not run ahead for I am not there. Be patient and wait for Me to move. I will tell you when it is time to move and when it is time to wait. Know that I am the Lord your God and I know what is best for you. I will not allow your enemy to destroy you if you seek Me with all your heart, listen to Me and are obedient to My will. I know your desire is to live in My will and be obedient. I know you seek My face. I know your heart. I know the depth of your soul's desires. In the days ahead I will satisfy your desires, but there are specific things that must be worked out first. There may be delays, but it will come. Be patient and wait for My timing. As you sit before Me in the quiet hours of the morning, I will reveal My plans to you ahead of time. You will know My heart, so you will be prepared. Be aware of the schemes of your enemy to get you off track. If you stay before Me and seek My face you will not fall into his traps."

$\approx$

"The Lord your God is forever, and He is full of blessings. Contentment and peace are found only in Me. I will rescue you from the depth of trials and temptations. I will set your feet upon a rock. I will take you to the high places. I will carry you when you are too weak to walk. I will provide for you in the midst of darkness. Poverty will not fall upon your bones. Surely, goodness and mercy will be yours forever."

$\approx$

"Child, you have moved into a place in My heart that not many will go because they are not willing to spend the time it takes to get there. It takes time to work through things to find the freedom that is only found in Me. I know you are willing to spend time with Me, since I have your permission to search deep within you, so that you might be free. I offer to you everything in the kingdom of Heaven you wish to obtain. Seek My face and you will receive My kingdom."

※

"The strength of the flesh, the power of the will, the human will, the human flesh — there is a battle going on and the flesh wants to win. But that is not My will in all of this. Pray against the flesh, rebuke the power it has, the strength and arrogance it carries. I want that broken. In order for Me to move, I need to break the flesh. Pray against the power your enemy has in your flesh. When it rises up it has power that can destroy. It's head means death unto the body. In order for the body to live the flesh must die. My will must prevail. Pray My will into being. Pray that you will be an overcomer. Your prayers can bring my will into being. Usher Me in. Permit Me into your midst, for I will not push My way in. I will not come in if I am not welcome. Allow Me to come in and guide you. Persevere. Persevere. Persevere."

※

"When you try to fix things on your own, that is when you feel discouraged and downtrodden. That is when your enemy comes in and attacks you and convinces you that you are no good. I want you to stop trying to do things on your own, for I never intended for you to fix things on your own. It was never meant for you to do this. Open your arms and let Me fill you."

※

"I want you to know My plans, My ways, My will, My purpose. I want to reveal My heart to you. I love you, child. I want to be in your life, your heart, and your spirit. Break the curse of dramatization and the reactionary spirit that lives within you. I want My spirit to have authority over that area of your life. Give up all that is within you and give it to Me. Relinquish the power and authority of your flesh to Me. Oh child, meet with Me face to face. As I met with Moses; so too I will meet with you. I yearn and long to have an intimate relationship with you. I want you to know Me, not just know about Me."

❧

"The treasures you seek are not of this world, because you cry out as Solomon did for wisdom and not for the riches of the world. Your heart's desire will be given unto you tenfold. The things you have not cried out for will also be given to you because you seek Me first and not the treasures of this world. I will restore to you the land you lost."

❧

"I want your life and your will. I want everything dear to you. I want your security to be found in Me and Me alone, not in a job, a person, education, or anything else. Seek Me first and I will give all the other things to you. Seek My heart and I will reveal My secrets to you. Lay before Me without ulterior motives, but only to know My will for your life and to know My secrets. Let My Spirit fall on you and have His way with you. I will take you into the heavenlies and reveal My secrets to you. I love you."

❧

"Do not add one more item to your already busy schedule. Sit and rest and listen to what I have to say to you. My greatest desire is that you sit and spend time with Me. When you go places and do things without My anointing, you will not accomplish that which you intended to do. Erase the schedule and start over. Let Me tell you where to go and what to do. My greatest desire is to spend time with you."

❧

"Each of you has different mountaintops. You will not all go to the same mountaintop. You will all arrive at different times. Do not think that just because someone else is experiencing a mountaintop that you will experience it also. I have each of you on a specific and special mountaintop. You will be satisfied there and your thirst will be quenched. There is a storm brewing, so it is important to know how to get to your mountaintop before the storm comes. I have given you advanced warning so you will know where the mountaintop is and how to get there. You must be able to go there in an instant. It is a place of rest from the storm. It is a place of refuge."

❧

"Let Me be your encourager when things look dreary. When situations look overpowering; they will not overpower you with Me. I am a place of refuge. I want you to come to this place everyday. As you run into My arms and crawl up on My lap, let Me be your refuge and encourager. The only way you will get through this time is to go hand in hand with Me, since in your own strength you cannot make it. It is not possible. Because you were never meant to do it all alone. Since I am the One who created the path you are to walk, I know all the places that could cause you to stumble. Embrace Me. It is okay to weep. You do not have to be strong. Lay down and let Me hold you and embrace you. Your heart has been deeply wounded. Run into My arms and let Me love you."

❧

"The new beginning will wipe out the sorrow and sadness you have endured getting to this point. No one will rob you of this joy. In this world you will continue to experience hardships, but take heart for I have conquered the world."

❧

"You say, 'the Lord has left me. He does not hear me anymore. He has gone away from me.' Child, I am where you let go of My hand. Seek Me. Come back to the place where you once were in fellowship with Me, in a love relationship with Me. Child, I miss you. Come and run into My arms this day. Let Me embrace you. Let Me love you. I do hear you but I cannot answer you because of where you are. Come take My hand and let's walk together once again. Come, seek My face for I miss you."

❧

"I want to pour out a tenderness upon My people. Are you ready for the hardness that you possess to be gone? Are you ready for your hurts to flee? Are you ready to see the changes for which you have longed? I am sending My Spirit to set you free from the chains that hold you and the bondages you have held on to for a long, long time. If you get serious with Me, I will get serious with you.

❧

"I want to remove the welts from the beatings you have received. All traces will be removed. They have caused calluses, bruises, hatred and bitterness to cover and protect them. But I will wipe all those things away. All of that will be gone and in the past."

❧

"The warfare is very real. The seriousness of the things the disciples went through and the apostles faced, you too will face. This is because of the growth you want to see and the things for which you have asked. The warfare you will face will appear to bring destruction, but in reality it will bring growth. Therefore, it is important for you to draw away into the secret place and to enter into this place within seconds. Get very familiar with doing this. In this secret place, I will speak to you as I spoke to Moses from the burning bush. I'll part the Red Sea for you if you will call upon Me and seek My face to find out what is really happening within each situation. I have parted the Red Sea and you have walked through it without destruction and without loss of life in the past, and I will do it again. Rejoice and know God is your Father and your Protector."

❧

"To a measure which is given, a measure will be required. Counting the cost is necessary for the next step to take place. In giving up everything, a hundredfold will be given back. Release everything to Me. Lay it all in My hands and do not take it back. Lay it down and see the majesty that comes from giving it to Me. I warn you in advance that a cost will be required of you. However, it is not to be feared. You will always be permitted to explain or give reasons for what you do. There will be a time when your mouth will be closed and you will not be permitted to speak because of the details I will be telling you. A time will lapse between giving up and getting back. More than days and months will pass where you will stand in a place and not be permitted to speak. I will tell you when this time is approaching. During this time, there will be no loss of life, only vision for those who try to find their vision through you. The price you will pay is to prepare you for humility so you may be used by your Father."

❧

"I am waiting on a generation to walk in My path. One who will go and walk in the anointing. There are not many who will give up everything to walk into the depth that I have prepared. It is not because I have not called, it is because not many will respond. I have been longing for you to get to this point. Your past has fulfilled a purpose. I had to get you to a place of maturity. Get ready for changes to come. You will see miracles. You will see legs grow. You will see cancer destroyed and brain tumors gone. When the doctors send them home to die and there is no hope, I will send them into your arms. Go; speak to these infirmities. When all else fails that is when I will come and do the work. I want to remove all doubt that it was the medical field that healed them. I want My name to be lifted up. When there is nothing left, I will send My Spirit."

≈

"Be reconciled with yourself and your past. Be liberated from the bondage of your past — the sins, turmoil and hatred. Receive My forgiveness and My freedom from those things. If you will release forgiveness and blessings to those who have hurt you, you will be set free. You will grow in leaps and bounds. Do you enjoy clinging to these things? Confess and repent for the day is short. Do you really want to be set free? Turn your face from the very thing you embrace which keeps you in bondage. This keeps you under the control of the one you do not want to control you. I tell you life comes when you rid yourselves of those things in your life that keep you bound up. Do you seek life? Then seek My face. Seek My will, My guidance, My love. In Me is where the peace and contentment you search for is found."

≈

"I want you to know that I am doing some pruning in your life, but do not be discouraged by it. If I did not love you, I would not prune you. I am making you into a firm, solid tree with big, deep roots. You will be one who will stand against the wind."

❧

"What is it you seek? What is your heart's desire this day? Child, come and speak from your heart. What frustrates you? What tires you? Bring them to Me. Pack them up in a box or suitcase and bring them to Me. Leave this baggage at My feet. Let Me deal with all these things. All you need to do is fix your eyes, thoughts, mind, and will upon Me and I will give you peace and rest. You can rescue no one. You cannot save anything. You cannot make it right. Only I can do these things. Only I can fix what is wrong and put these things in their rightful place. Run to Me. Do not hesitate any longer for surely you will die trying to make them right. Lay them down and I will give you rest."

❧

"The victory is yours. The battle is won. Believe in your heart that you are the victors. With Me as your Savior, you have already overcome the battle that desires to tear you down. Your enemy is a liar when he tells you that you are not overcomers. So, therefore, you must know you are overcomers."

❧

"You are about to enter into a new thing. As Abraham had a waiting season to grow and mature, so did you. Now is the time to walk on, to walk into the reason I have created you. The past has been for a time such as this and its purpose will be revealed in what I am about to do. I am about to move you to another place, another level, another realm of My love. You have been a child and you have done things as a child, now that time of your life is over. Now you will eat meat, no more soft food. Move into new things. Readily embrace all that I bring your way. I will protect you from your enemy. You will learn to cast out sickness. You will go to the depths of the wishing well with Me. Never again to return to what you now know. Release all you are and all you have into Me, then we will begin. We will go on a journey of celebration. Never return to this place again. Your wisdom and knowledge will increase. You will know and see things very few people will ever know or see. This is not because I love you more, but because of your obedience to go and do these things. Your willingness to know Me and do My will is what takes you to the depths."

❧

"The sun rises and falls on your days but I tell you My love is ever constant. There is no rising or falling in My love for you. You are My child. In all things trust your Father. For I do have reasons for all things and in all things I am working and building My kingdom in you. For I know your desire is to be filled with who I am. Surely you will know My presence, you will see My face, you will hold My hand and stand beside Me all the days of your life."

❧

"My changes in your life are like you changing your furniture around in different seasons. This is a new and different season and it is time for rearranging. Just stand in it. It is not to be feared. It is not meant to be painful. It is refreshing when you move furniture around, so too, this will be refreshing when it is finished. It is a good thing. Do not fear it. Simply rest in it."

❧

"Your growth will come quickly because My Spirit is upon you to teach you what is in My heart. I want you to be ready for change in your life. It won't be as you expect it to be, but it will be good. It will be better than you could ever imagine. I am placing deep desires within your heart. You will stand in awe of what I am about to do. It will all unfold in a matter of time. Out of the blue it will appear. I tell you this to encourage you and to reassure you it is from Me, for I am the Lord your God. All things are found in Me. I am your provider. I am your gatekeeper and the gate is about to open and floods from Heaven will pour out."

❧

"I hear you say, 'I wish you would speak My name.' I say to you, not only am I going to speak your name, but I also want to tell you how much I love you. I want to embrace you. Can you feel my embrace? Lean back, rest in My arms, and let Me embrace you. It is important for you to feel My embrace since I want you to allow Me to be in control of all things. You cannot do it, but I can. Lay back in My arms and let Me be in control."

❧

"Things will soon be finalized. Stand firm. Stand your ground so you do not lose what you have fought for. Major changes will take place. Be confident that I am the Lord your God and that I have all things under My control. Look and see the light shining. There are joyous times ahead. Blessings will flow from all avenues. Wait and stand in what you know. Do not compromise what you believe for anyone. Stand firm and wait patiently on Me to move things around. Stand in the midst of it all. Enjoy where you are, smile, laugh and be joyous, for your Father in Heaven is in control. I know all things. I see all things."

❧

"Do not fear what the world dishes out. I have you in the palm of My hand. You are Mine and I will keep you safe. You are My beloved and I love you."

❧

"The water is deep and there is much to be had by you. Plenty will be laid upon the table. Out of nowhere it will appear and for no apparent reason except that you are My beloved child and I adore you. As we walk along the beach, My arm of comfort is around your shoulder. I whisper words of love to you and you find rest and peace in Me. In My presence there is no fear, there is no turmoil."

❧

"Come to Me at all times and I will bring you rest and comfort for I am the Lord your God, your Father in whom you trust. Seek after righteousness all the days of your life and you will be blessed. Know this, in My love all things are made right. All things are made perfect. In My love all things come together. When you labor in My love, nothing else matters."

❧

"You see your problems and situations as great, big, enormous— even huge. Nothing you face is too big for Me. As the people marched around the wall of Jericho and commanded it to fall, you too need to command your walls to fall. The wall was built brick by brick with all the protection you could build into it. Tell it to come down and it will come down. For I am the Lord your God and I want to tear down walls that were built to keep Me out. I want to set you free from the bondages of hate, turmoil, and torment. Be free in Me."

❧

"Pick up your sword and run into battle. When you do, you will have My strength. Do not give into what your enemy says about defeat. He will tell you that you will be defeated because he knows you will be victorious. The opposite of what your enemy tells you is the truth. Move on in the confidence of the Lord, knowing you are victorious."

❧

"There is only one solution to your struggles, turmoil, and torment and yet you run aimlessly into the darkness looking for answers. If you will run into the light, into the arms of Jesus, you will find peace, joy, and answers to your questions."

≫

"Get ready for the great violent wind of the Holy Spirit as the disciples experienced in the book of Acts. It will be as a new breath of freshness, a depth where you have never been. It will take you miles down the road in your relationship with Me. You have gone through the past for what is about to happen."

≫

"You have the faith to move mountains. It is deep within you. As you pray for the sick, you will see miracles. Just a simple prayer takes you to your Father's heart. Your faith runs deep like an ocean, miles and miles in depth. Seek after Me and do My will and watch the miracles take place."

≫

"You truly want freedom but you hide behind a veil of fear. This fear is the condemnation your enemy has placed upon you. It is meant to keep you from knowing Me. Walk through the veil for the freedom you seek is on the other side. Take that step of faith and walk through the veil to the freedom you fear, and yet at the same time, long to have. Don't wait. Don't put it off any longer. The longer you wait, the harder it will be. Do not look to the left, to the right, or to the people beside you, but look straight ahead into the eyes of your Heavenly Father."

❧

"I, the Lord, stand before you with outstretched arms. Run into them. Seek what you need today. Weep and weep and weep until there is nothing left. Ask for the things you need. Seek those blessings. You seek after joy and happiness in others, but I want to be your joy. I will begin to interrupt your life. I am going to speak with increased intensity. Sit and listen for My voice."

❧

"I stand before you. Do you see My face? Can you feel My presence? I hear your cries. I see your pain, hurts, frustrations, and anxiety. I stand with My arms stretched out ready to embrace you. Reach out to Me. Do you need love and forgiveness? I release these to you. The problems you carry are not yours to carry. You were never meant to carry them. Release them to Me. I will carry them for you. I have the answers you need and are looking for. The bondages that held you back are now being broken. You look at situations and think, that used to bother Me, but now it doesn't. I am working things out in your life. Be encouraged and know I am not done. We will continue until all is broken and released from your life. You are not a hopeless or helpless people, for I am your God and I will not leave you the way you are. I love you. You are My beloved."

❧

"I will place My blessing upon My people. Watch and see how Great and Mighty is the Lord your God. Fall down and worship only Me. Great is the Lord and greatly to be praised. I am concerned about the church, the health of the body of My Son. There are ailments that need to be healed. My hands are tied unless the church is willing to give them up. Release them into the arms of My Son. Allow these things to fall to the ground. Do not permit them to be an issue any longer. They cause a separation between us. Your clothes are soiled and need to be made spotless, as the Lamb is spotless. Repent and allow My Son to cleanse and heal you. For you are His bride and you need to be made pure, whole and spotless. Guard you hearts, for evil men wish to steal and devour them. Watch and be aware of the one who wants to snatch your life. Be aware of the schemes and plots he has to kill you. Draw close to the One who gives you wisdom and understanding and you will be protected."

❧

"Guard yourselves from the temptations of old. Your Father has saved you from the torment and death of your sins. Be cautious not to turn back and embrace them. At times it may seem easier, but I tell you this will surely bring death. Run into My arms when you are tempted to return to old things. Safety and protection are in My arms alone. Do not turn to the world for wisdom or answers, for they will surely advise you to go to the things of your past. The world's counsel is to embrace the sins of your past. Keep your eyes focused on Me."

❧

"A time is coming when the blessings of your Father will be poured out among you. If you stand true to your faith, you will receive your portion. If you turn from Me, your portion will be withheld from you. Your eyes have seen and your ears have heard of Me and the mighty things I have done. Walk in faith, believing for the things you do not yet see and they will be bestowed upon you. My hand holds many blessings, but wrath also comes to those who turn from Me. Walk in uprightness. Walk in humility, faith, and patience believing in the Lord your God and life will be yours in the kingdom of Heaven."

❧

"Are you weary, weak, worn out and tired? Do you feel you do not have enough strength to take one more step? Begin to walk in My strength. Embrace Me and walk in My power. As you look back to other rough times in your life, you will see that I carried you through them. Just look into My eyes and let Me be your strength."

❧

"Your past is your past. Do not permit your enemy to bring it up in guilt and shame. When you asked for forgiveness, you were forgiven. If you need to take a bag and place all your past in it and bury it, then do so. Your past is not your present. It is your past. Your enemy wants to steal your peace, joy and hope that comes with forgiveness.

Do not let this happen. I want you set free from this so you can move forward."

❧

"You are not defeated, all is not lost. Look up and see the Son smiling at you. Do you see My arms opened to you? Do not hang your head to the ground, for all you will see is darkness. When you look up to the Heavens, into the sun, you will see Me. Know that you are victorious. Victory belongs to you. Do not let your enemy tell you otherwise. Do not try to quench your desires that can only be quenched by more of Me. The more you attempt to satisfy these with your flesh, the less satisfied you will be."

❧

"You were not a mistake or a surprise to your Father. I do not make mistakes. You have been beaten and down-trodden most of your life. I know your comings and goings, your past and your future, and I still love you with an everlasting love."

❧

"Do not take sides. You are divided because your enemy has convinced you that you are right. You have moved from walking in the Spirit to walking in the flesh. You have decided you have the right to judge and point fingers. You are consumed by thoughts of hatred. It is all you can do to survive because your thoughts are controlled by the good and bad. When you hate your brothers, you see flesh and not spirit. You have moved away from the Lord your God when you do this. You have put on boxing gloves, but you are fighting the wrong enemy. Satan stands back and laughs at you because you have swallowed his lie. Fall on your face and repent for you have sinned. Power comes when you are bound together in one accord."

❧

"The events in your life are part of a process. You will know who is for you and who is against you. The Lord your God is for you. Stand firm and pray, then move on. Do not allow these things to keep you down. The wind will blow but it will not break you. If you look through your spiritual eyes you will see it is only the wind blowing. You will survive. You will survive."

❧

"Face your fears. Battle with what seeks to conquer you. What is standing in your way? What is blocking the doorway? What is it that causes chills to go up and down your spine? What is it that causes you to say, 'anything but that Lord'? What is it that causes you to turn around and walk in the other direction? What is it that haunts you? Time and time again you turn away and feel defeated. Who or what is your Goliath? What is it that you want the Lord your God to deliver into your hands? Run into the face of your enemy. Meet it face to face."

❧

"Allow Me to soften your heart for the world has taken its toll. Allow Me to touch your heart and bring peace to your soul. The turmoil is more than you can stand. Only My love can come and take away the darkness that has crept in. Let Me lighten the load that has been placed upon you. It weighs you down to the point where you just want to lay down and die. Let me walk with you through this. Take My hand and walk with Me. I will guard and guide you all your days; for you are My beloved."

✣

"There are two ways to choose. Two separate paths from which to pick. It is a time of decision making for you. As you seek My face, I will reveal what path you should walk down. You know which path is right, but a part of you wants to walk a different path. I will give you the strength to stay true to the right path. Seek My face and I will be found by you."

✣

"You do not go unnoticed by your Father. Much of your life you have gone unnoticed by men, but I tell you I know you by name. Do not give up. Do not quit. I see you and I love you. Even though you may not have visible signs of my presence, I am right beside you."

✣

"Rejoice, rejoice when you are persecuted by the world, for truly you are My beloved. Be at peace. Be content in My love. Know that all things work together for the good of those who love Me. I will provide all that you need, so do not fear. For surely I tell you fear comes from your enemy. He has come to steal your peace and joy. Be silent to those who persecute you. For a time is coming when all will see the hand of your Father working in your behalf so do not try to redeem yourself. Watch your actions and attitudes. Stand silent yet firm while the stones are being thrown. It will only last a short time then My will can surface and prevail. My hand overpowers the hand of your enemy. The enemy has spoken, but I have not yet spoken. Miracles will come from the destruction meant by your enemy. Your obedience has been noticed. Your Father will interrupt the schemes of men. Watch them fall by the wayside. They will disappear into the ground as raindrops do. They have had their say. I have not yet spoken. Wait patiently for My voice. Then and only then will the earth be moved and your enemy will run and scatter to the ends of the earth looking for a place to hide. Stand in My shadow and wait for My hand to move. Your enemy is sure he has given you a death sentence. But your Father will not permit it. There is true life in this presumed death sentence. Wait. Sit and wait for My hand to move."

⤲

"Your dreams will reveal the direction you are to take. I, the Lord your God, will separate those who can walk it out and those who cannot. The times ahead will be kept for the fit. Not necessarily physically fit, but spiritually fit. Stand true to your God. Stand firm in the winds for truly they are only winds. Winds that have been permitted to blow for I knew you would withstand them. You will be safe and stronger at the end of them."

❧

"If you want people's lives to be changed, then speak blessings into their lives and not curses. Bless them in the name of the Lord your God. Speak blessings into their lives. When blessings fall from your mouth, their hearts and yours will be changed."

❧

"If you will believe in Me and trust Me, I will provide everything I have promised. All things come through My hands."

❧

"Great warfare, for your lives, is taking place in the heavenlies. Your enemy is fighting harder than ever before to destroy you and the land you have gained. Stand firm. Stand tall, not in arrogance and pride, but in assurance of who you are in Me."

❧

"Hush My child, for once again the sun will rise and bring warmth into your soul. Once again you will smell the fragrance of the flowers after a summer's rain. Once again the trees will have blossoms that sparkle and shine and call your name as you pass by. They will dance in the breeze provided to bring a coolness to you."

≥

"I reveal My plans to My people. To those who will listen, I will share My thoughts. Today is the beginning of new beginnings. This is the tip of the iceberg, the first of many firsts. You will be involved in what I am doing. I have chosen you and called you by name. I have hand picked each one of you. All of you have different talents and gifts that are to compliment one another. No one is any more important than the other. For surely a day is coming when you will sit with the bridegroom. What men have to say about you is not always the truth. I have called you and chosen each one of you. You are all hand picked by My Father. Rejoice in this. Know that you are fulfilling the visions and the dreams of your Father that He has placed in your hearts. You were called for a time such as this."

≥

"Do not wait to release forgiveness to those who have hurt you. For the day is coming when it will be too late. Do not let your enemy rob you any longer. Understand who is your real enemy."

≥

"At times, it is easier to believe for others than for yourself. I love you just as I love others. No one is inferior to another in My eyes. I am not a respecter of persons. It is easier for you to accept that I love others more than I love you. That is not the truth. Do not look at the gifts others have and decide I love them more. I love you just as I love them. Do not fall in love with the gifts they have, fall in love with the Giver of the gifts."

❧

"If you will prepare a place for Me to come and sit, I will dwell among you and never leave. My protection is all around you. I will not allow anyone or anything to stop My will from being done in your life. I refuse to allow your enemy to interfere with your life at this time. I have a purpose that needs fulfilled. The timing is right and nothing will stand in My way. Walk through this. Persevere during this time, My beloved."

❧

"Do not strive to find Me, for I sit right beside you. I have not been separated from you. I place My face against your face, My nostrils against your nostrils, My cheek against your cheek. I desire for you to breathe in the very breath that I exhale. My desire for My church is to have the same breath that I have, no space between us, no difference. I exhale; you inhale. Let out all the old and breathe in the fresh breath of the Lord your God. Stop striving to bring things to pass. I have shown you time and time again that I will provide in all things both big and small. I am the Lord your God and it is time for you lay down all your schemes to get rich quick. Just trust Me to take care of you, for I love you and I will not let you go without the things you need to do the things I have called you to accomplish. I am a good God. I am faithful in all things. Watch and wait and again you will see how I will take care of you."

"You have been given many promises and if they were not so I would have told you. You can trust Me. I will let you know when they are not truth."

"I stand before you, open your spiritual eyes and see Me. As I stand before you, I ask you an age old question, one that I have asked you before. Will you follow Me and Me alone? Will you serve Me and Me alone? I know that you said yes before, but you had not counted the cost at that time. Now that you have counted the cost, will you answer yes again? What is your answer? I stand and wait on your response."

"My beloved, how I long for you to see Me as your friend and not as your judging King. I want you to grasp My hands and seek My face. Let Me sit beside you and converse with you. I want to commune with you. Look at Me in a different manner, for I desire you to see Me as your friend. My desire is to sit with you and love you as a friend. I love you, beloved. I love you."

"I have showers of blessings for My children. My basket is over flowing with peace, joy, hope and faith. You must reach out and catch them. I will not permit you to be satisfied with what the world has to offer. That void can only be filled by Me."

⚶

"The rejection you have experienced from the world is not a reflection of your worth and value to Me. It does not reflect how much I love you, since you have yet to experience the depth and magnitude of My love. Do not settle for anything less than all of the love I have to give you. Go to the mountaintop, not halfway up the mountain. My love is crisp and fresh and new every morning. Come to the source of true love. Come to the throne and climb up on My lap. Let Me reveal true love to you. You have been bruised, broken, and beaten by those around you. Do not look to others for wholeness. Look to Me, let Me fulfill you. Do not seek from the world what I alone can give you."

⚶

"I want to reveal My heart to you. I want to draw you unto Me and give you rest. I want you to walk in peace and tranquility all your days. When you are close to Me, peace overflows for that is what I am. In all things give thanks. There is victory in a thankful heart. I want you to walk in the confidence that you belong to Me. You are My beloved."

⚶

"You have touched only a small portion of what I have for you. I will withhold nothing from you. Everything I have and everything I am can be sought after by you. If you will come after Me, I will meet you."

❧

"Search for Me while I may be found by you, for a time will come when all is quiet. You will not feel My presence, but you will and must know I am with you. Many things are changing. There are many things I wish to tell you. Do not be shocked or surprised by what I have to say. Sit and listen to what is on My heart."

❧

"Where does your treasure lie? Where is your strength found? To whom do you run for help? Let Me be your Guide. You are chosen and consecrated for My service, not the world. Stand apart from the world as the statue of liberty. She stands alone in the ocean. Set apart from every country, she makes a stand for peace, freedom, and liberty. Her strength, stability, and steadfastness is from a firm, solid, and strong foundation."

❧

"Let truth be the center of your life. In all you say and do, let truth be there in the midst. Reactions, attitudes and decisions need to be made in truth. Do not strive; be who I made you."

≈

"There are many changes that lie ahead of you. Keep your eyes focused on Me and you will know which way to turn and what to do. If you stay focused on Me, you will not be caught off guard or lose your footing. The days ahead are meant to bring you into deep communion with Me. Everything you have walked through has been to get you to this point. If it had been easy, you would not have gotten to this place. The times I pushed you were for your own good. As you reflect on them, you will agree there was no easy way to get you to this point. Fall deeper in love with Me. Do not chase after other things. Release your spirit to Me."

≈

"Many of the roads you traveled were crossroads to get you to this point. At those crossroads decisions had to be made. Some roads were traveled over again so different decisions could be made. As you were being prepared for this place, this place was being prepared for you. It is time for you to take your position. Open the door and step into this new place."

≈

"Disappointments have overcome you. They have enveloped you. You stand with fists clenched in anger. Unclench your fists, open your arms and reach out for Me. I want to pick you up. I love you. I have not left you, nor have I forsaken you. I stand beside you. Step into My arms."

❧

"I call you to obedience. Step out of your comfort zone. Stop doing things to please others, for it is not pleasing to Me. You stop My blessings when you do not follow through with what I have asked you to do. When you walk in obedience you unlock the door to the banquet room."

❧

"The rejection you have felt from the world is not a reflection of your worth and value to Me. It does not reflect how much I love you. You have yet to experience the depth and magnitude of My love for you. Do not settle for less. Go to the top of the mountain. People in your life have not always done a good job of reflecting my love. Come to the source. Come to My throne and climb on My lap. Let Me reveal true love and true acceptance to you. Wholeness comes from Me, not men. You have been bruised and broken by those around you. Look only to Me, the One and Only God of Heaven and Earth. Be fulfilled in Me, not the world. Do not seek from them what I alone can give you."

❧

"The spoken word comes from whatever lies within your heart. Speak words of life and not death. Speak words of prosperity, not poverty. Speak of winning, not losing. Whatever is good and righteous, think on these things and speak of these things."

❧

"I want to reveal My heart to you. I want to be intimate with you. I want to reveal My love to you. Draw nigh unto Me and I will give you rest. Walk in peace and tranquility all your days. When you are close to Me, peace overflows for that is who I am. In all things, give thanks, for there is power in a thankful heart. There is victory over many things when you walk in a thankful heart. Walk in faith. Walk in knowing who your Father is and where your victory comes from."

❧

"What is it you fear? Why do you fear it? Change is how I bring My will into being. Do not fret about what could happen. Search for Me and you will find Me. Ask for peace and I will deliver it. Look to me for the answers you need. Seek after Me with your whole heart and I will give you rest."

❧

"Just as quickly as the storms come, they also pass. Some are fierce and some are mild. No matter what the circumstance is that surrounds your life, I want you to know My steadfast love. I want you to have peace and be calm in the midst of the storm. Be still and know that I am God. I am the same yesterday, today and forever."

❧

"Do not strive to know Me, simply be still. Sit quietly and listen for My voice, for I have much to say to you. I am your friend and I want to sit and visit with you. I want to be involved with every aspect of your life. When you strive to feel My presence, when you strive to see Me, when you strive to touch Me, you miss Me. Jump in the water. I am there. Just jump in."

❧

"There is change in the air. Great and mighty things are about to take place. Get ready. Excitement fills the heavenlies."

❧

"If you think for one minute that you are insignificant in the kingdom of Heaven, you are believing lies. I created every one of My children for a purpose. None were a mistake and none were a surprise to Me. If you have not caught a glimpse of your purpose, then chase after Me until you do. For if you do not fulfill the purpose that I created for you, then something is missing in My Kingdom. I created you and I know all about you. Others may have thrown you away or they may not want you, but this is not true in My Kingdom. Turn from that thought and know it comes from your enemy. You are My beloved. I created you for a time such as this. You are not small or insignificant in My Kingdom."

❧

"I am a God who redeems, redeeming those who have been wronged. A season of redeeming has begun. Stand in the midst of accusation. Stand firm in truth and I will redeem you, for I am Truth. If you remain in Me, I will remain in you. I, Truth, will prevail. Have faith. Have patience. Forbid your enemy entrance into your camp. Crush your enemy under your feet."

❧

"You may be in a place where you feel helpless, but you serve a risen King who is not helpless. Do not look at the place where you are, but look to Whom you belong. Look above and beyond where you are, to where you are going to be when I am done with you. Place yourself in the shadow of My wings. This is where your power and strength come from. If you are trying to gain the strength to fight this fight on your own, you will never do it. If you are fighting your own battle you will fail. The battle belongs to the Lord your God."

❧

"In the midst of the rain there is a rainbow. It is a sign of hope, a sign of peace. A sign that I am with you at all times. Do not give up hope. Never lose sight of the fact that I am with you through all things. In all things seek My face."

❧

"If I am for you, who can be against you? If you are doing My will, the giants will fear you. If you are doing what I am doing, your enemy will flee."

❧

"Let freedom flow. Let your praise be heard from the mountaintop. Let your heart sing. Let your spirit be set free to praise. When you praise Me, the heavens are opened and miracles are released. Do not let your lips be sealed by the hardships you endure. Break through; open your mouth and let the praises from within you flow."

❧

"I say stand in the midst of the wind. You will find change that is good and righteous. Change that I have promised you long ago."

❧

"It is time for you to move into a new place. It is a new dimension, a new level. Take My hand and lets walk into this new place together. Let Me lead you through the door. I will show you the way."

❧

"Here I am waiting. Abide in Me. Here I am longing for you. Hide in My love. Here I stand with My arms wide open. Run into them."

❧

"Do you love to love Me? Sit on My lap and let Me caress your face. Lay your head on My shoulder and hear the words of love I have to share with you. I am the breath of fresh air you have been waiting for."

❧

"Have eyes that see and ears that hear My voice. Receive the treasures I have to give to you. Receive them with open arms and a willing heart. Do not step back from them. I am the giver of good gifts, and freely give as an example for you to follow. Take - for I am giving. Receive because I have great plans for you to fulfill. Do you wish to know Me? You must partake of the gifts I have for you. I will give you a heart that will follow whole-heartedly with complete devotion. This is a desire you have had deep within you for a long time."

❧

"I have given you dreams and visions that have not yet come to pass. Do not let anyone or anything steal these from you. Some may appear absurd and far off, but you know deep within your spirit that I have told you these things. Cling to them. Let them bring you peace and joy while you await their arrival."

❧

"Your thoughts and your ways are not mine. You have been judgmental. Repent of wanting your way. You are my beloved bride and I know what is best for you. My timing is perfect."

❧

"You have entered into the throne room and have touched My heart. As you continue to seek My face, you will stand in the midst of every situation and know that victory will come to pass."

❧

"Do not settle for the gifts that you have today. In My kingdom there is so much more for you to experience. There is a bigger picture than what you have been shown. There is so much more light to shine on your path. What you think is awesome, is only a stepping-stone to where I will take you. You have yet to see My greatest miracle take place in your life. There is so much more to come, so do not become complacent in your position. Seek more of Me. There is much more to come. Watch, look, and seek for Me while I may be found by you."

❧

"Have you forgotten the first time I called you by name? Have you forgotten the first time you felt My embrace and kiss upon your cheek? Have you forgotten the times I walked with you through the dark valley and the shadow of death? Have you forgotten the times that I carried you through hurts and trials? This time in your life is no different from the rest. I have not left you, nor have I forsaken you. I stand beside you. I stand with you and not against you. This time, as all others, shall surely pass away. You will see the end of the tunnel. The sun will rise once again."

❧

"When I give a promise to you, take it as if it is done, already accomplished. For I speak from what has already taken place. It will surely come to pass. When you eat physical food, you must chew it up and swallow it. The same is true with My word. Take it into your spirit. Make it part of your very being and live in it. Live each day in the promises that I have given to you and you will possess peace, joy, hope and love."

❧

"If your situations or circumstances appear dark, bleak and out of control, look up and see My face. Look into My eyes. Do not look down, for there you will only see more darkness and despair. Look up to the heavens and seek My face. There is hope, joy, peace, "Sonshine", warmth and love to be found by you. The situation is not as it appears. When you look upward, you will find the answers you seek. There is comfort for which you long. Run into My arms, let Me pour out My love to you."

❧

"I will not let you run from being rejected by others. If you do not stand in the midst of the rejection, you cannot learn from it and move into the deeper place. There is rejection from the world as well as those closest to you, even within the church. It will intensify. It will keep you in a state of humility."

❧

"Stop the rush of your life. Smell the fragrance that lingers in your midst. It is My fragrance. It is My call to you to sit and sup with me. Do you feel the peace as My presence lingers? I have come to sit with you, to be in your midst. I stand before you, breathe in the fresh breath that I bring to you. Inhale a deep breath and exhale the stale breath that lies within you. I have come to take the heaviness from you, if you will give it to Me. I will take the weight from your shoulders so you can find rest. I adore you child. I have chosen you to be Mine. Will you run into My arms and let Me bring My comfort to you?"

❧

"You must understand that independence and freedom are the opposite of one another. Independence takes you from My realm of safety and into the enemy's camp. It leaves you unguarded for the world to tempt you. But, I tell you that freedom brings you into a deeper realm of My love. Freedom lets you stand hand in hand with Me. Your flesh will go after independence and it will lead you to death. Freedom will bring you into the kingdom of Heaven. Which will you choose?"

❧

"Focus your attention on Me. Victory lies in Me, so concentrate on Me. Time is of the essence. Look to Me for direction. Your path in life lies in Me. The journeys I have for you rely on you seeking after Me for guidance. I will lead you, but you must be obedient to follow Me. I must be the head and you must learn to be My hands and My feet."

❧

"It is time for you to take a step deeper into My kingdom. A new place awaits you. Leap off the mountain. Step out of the comfort zone you have built for yourself. Fly high as an eagle. Set your sights on a new realm. I have exciting places for you to go and exhilarating things for you to experience. Are you willing to step out? Are you willing to let Me take you to a new place in My kingdom? I await your response."

❧

"I, the Lord, save you from your enemies. I am the One who delivers you into a place of safety. I destroy your foes. I make your adversaries to bow down. I come to liberate you. I come to set you free from the bondage that holds you captive. Break down the walls of judgment and condemnation. I have come to set you free. Today, true freedom in Me awaits you."

❧

"Do not get caught off guard by the things that enter into your daily life. Stay focused on Me and I will take care of the stray bullets that are aimed at you by your enemy. Keep on track and stay on the path I prepared for you to walk. I will take care of the briars along the way. If you focus on the activity on either side of you, it will capture your attention away from Me. I will take care of you if you stay focused on Me."

☙

"A word has been innocently spoken that has attached itself to you. This negative word attached itself to your spirit and is destroying you from the inside out. You feel you were a burden. You have taken what was spoken and internalized it to be truth. You are very much in need of your Fathers' love. Allow Me to hold you and love you as you long to be loved by your Father."

☙

"Do not base your worth and value on what your earthly father thought of you. You were created with great worth and value. Look to your heavenly Father as your source of fulfillment. Do not let anything block the love relationship I desire to have with you. Many of you are living out the words spoken over you by the world. Break out of that mold that was placed around you long ago; realize that you were never meant to live in that. You were never created to walk through some of the things you have experienced. Come, run into My arms. I love you more than you could ever think possible. Lay down the self-condemnation and self-doubt of what you can and cannot be. I have a high calling for you. To be My child is a high calling - a great honor. To be in My arms is a wonderful place of rest."

❧

"To think you have little value is pride not humility. Walk on, walk the path I have created for you to walk. Take heed to the call that I have placed upon your life. I am widening the borders of your territory."

❧

"There are answers in the quietness that has come upon you at the present time. Silence will take you into a marvelous understanding of whom you are in Me, so keep walking in the silence. I will not let you miss Me in this time. I will lead you and guide you into your fullness. Remain steadfast in the midst of the silence and I will reveal My plan and purpose to you. This time of silence will take you into a deeper revelation of Me. Let Me have My way in your life. Lay prostrate before Me. Trust Me and you will find rest."

❧

"The timing of events is crucial. All things will fall into place when they are ordained by Me. Your vow and promise are sacred to Me. Do not be put on the defensive by your enemy, but rather work from a position of offense. Do not respond until you have clear direction from Me. Stand, wait and watch to see what I will do."

❧

"I love you because I created you. Nothing you could do could make me love you any more or any less. Enter into a deeper place within Me that you have never experienced before. A place of safety awaits you where no one or no thing can take anything from you."

⌇

"Let Me anoint your head with oil and renew your vow to Me. Let Me take you to the door post and pierce your ear. Live in My house all your days."

⌇

"I am about to overflow your cup. Once it begins to overflow there will be no holding back, like a dam breaking because of the force of the water. All the days of your life there will be an overflow of My blessings. No cup is big enough to hold what I have in store for you. I am sending this overflow from My storehouse where I have been keeping it for a time such as this. It will be withheld from you no longer."

⌇

"Come, let's dance in the meadow. Let's draw nigh to one another. Come out of your hiding place - your secret place. Let's stand before the multitudes. Let Me display My beloved bride in whom I am well pleased. Let Me remove the unrighteousness that has been your cloak for much too long. Let Me dress you with My righteousness and beauty. Come away with Me my beloved."

My Father's Voice

❧

"I have a new song to place in your heart: a new tune with new words. It will be new to your life but I have sung this song over you all your days. It will reveal to you the new tide, the new adventure I have in store for you. You have prevailed when it would have been easier for you to stop and turn back. You continued in the midst of strife. With no direction at hand you walked on. You are My beloved child."

❧

"I knew you before your conception. I held you first at your birth before handing you over to the doctor and then your parents. You were not a mistake to Me. I planned your birth. You were created by Me to fulfill My purpose. I marked you for Me and My kingdom."

❧

"Be careful not to compromise your stand. If you give an inch, your enemy will take a mile. Be cautious not to give in to pressure."

❧

"Whom do you serve? Whose opinion are you most concerned about? I am kind, loving and merciful. The world is cruel, imperfect, inconsistent and judgmental. If you focus your eyes on them, it will bring death and destruction to our relationship. Focus on Me. Let Me embrace you, forgive you, and envelop you with My arms. I love you with an everlasting love."

❧

"Do not taunt your enemy. Stop this practice and repent. Do not engage in presumptive behavior for this will bring death unto you. Fix your eyes on Me, not your enemy. Focus on Me and My will and My plans."

❧

"I am preparing a bride that is pure, crisp, white and clean; a bride without spot or wrinkle. That is what I am doing in you and all who will come after Me."

❧

"Do not fear those who speak against you, for you are my treasure and you belong to me. What I say about you is much different than what men may say, so remain silent in your response. There is nothing that needs to be said by you. I, the Lord your God, will provide for you and protect you from you enemies."

❧

"From where does your confidence come? Men or Me? I want to place My words deep within you. Do you have your own agenda? Let Me reveal My purpose for your life. Only one path will bring the peace and contentment that you long for. Come to Me. Your peace lies in Me."

❧

"Rise and shine for the day of the Lord has come. Now is the time to lend your ear to the word of the Lord. Put on the armor of the Lord. Prepare for battle. Place the armor where it belongs. Do not compromise one for another because it leaves an opening for your enemy to enter in."

❧

"I stand in front, beside, and behind you. I am your protector. I am the lover of your soul. Do you doubt that I exist? Are there times that you wonder if I am with you? Be assured that when you cry out to Me, I hear you. I know your voice. I know your name. I love you."

❧

"I desire a deeper walk with you, therefore, you must leave your comfort zone. There are many new things for you to experience. Where you have been has been good, but there is so much more. The passion you have is not fulfilling. I have placed a desire within you to seek after more of Me. If you will sit with Me, I will reveal the new path I have prepared for you."

❧

"Are you willing to lay down your life for Me? Will you look past the situation in order to see what is really happening? Things are not how they appear. When the day is the darkest, light is about to shine through. Will you hang on? Will you continue on in spite of how life appears? Will you trust Me when it would be easier to walk away? Do not give up. All is not lost. I am about to shine through the darkness. Your enemy has spoken a lie to distract you from seeking the truth. Look past the lie to see the truth. I am the Truth."

❧

"Who or what satisfies your spirit? Who or what do you chase after? Who or what has control of your life? What do you spend your time doing? Do you seek the One who satisfies? Do you chase after the One who longs for you? I am the Lord your God. I love you and long for you to come unto Me."

❧

"You search for truth. You search for instructions. You look from corner to corner for understanding. In your search look deep into the heart of your Father, for I am the Truth that you seek. I am the Way you wish to walk in. I am your all in all. I am the fountain that will quench your thirst. Will you drink from this fountain of truth? I will reveal to you the truth in your situations. You ask what is truth? It is in Me. Seek after Me. Search for Me while I may be found by you."

❧

"I am raising up an army on all sides of the earth, a great generation of warriors for the kingdom of heaven.

The world calls them useless, worthless, and unlovely. I call them Mine."

❧

"It is not an act that brings about a miracle. It is the condition of your heart. Obedience is better than sacrifice."

❧

"Be cautious of your own agenda. I have put a stop to those who walk alone trying to accomplish My will on their own. It takes the whole body working together in one accord for My return to take place. Walk together, hand in hand. Bind together in one accord, one mind, one spirit. Do not pull away from My body, My bride."

❧

"In order for you to enter into the new land, there are adjustments that must be made in your life. The day has come for you to choose what path you will follow. Restoration will come in accordance with My purpose. Flow in the river of love. The time has come for extreme measures. There is urgency for My people to be on the same page. Directional change is on the way. Serious change. Extreme change. There are things you hang on to that are not and will not be welcomed in this new place. Lay down the hindrances that keep you from going to this new place. Chase after Me. Seek Me. Love Me, for I love you."

❧

"Understand that I am stretching the faith that lies within you, since your faith is not being utilized to its fullest capacity. There is a depth you have not realized that lies within you. I am doing a work in you to get this new level of faith within you."

❧

"I have found you sitting weary, wasting away in the darkness of your room. You are tired; you have no strength to walk another mile. All you want is step out of life for a while. I stand before you and kneel down beside you. I pick you up and kiss your cheek. There is strength in My arms. I will make you new. For in your weakness, I am strong. My breath becomes your breath. My spirit consumes your spirit. No longer is it you living, but Me living in you."

❧

"Why do you fall in love with things that are not eternal? Reevaluate what you focus your time and attention on. Be filled with My Spirit. I am the One who can quench all desires with in you."

❧

"Seek Me. Be desperate for My presence. Worship Me. Fall in love with Me. I am a jealous God. I long for your attention."

"When brokenness happens in your hearts, openness appears in the heavens. It lays out a path for Me to reveal Myself to you. When you catch a glimpse of My holiness, you will never be the same."

To order additional copies of

My Father's
Voice

send $15.00 to

P. O. Box 362
Lisbon, Ohio 44432

www.ingramcontent.com/pod-product-compliance
Lightning Source LLC
Chambersburg PA
CBHW062026040426
42447CB00010B/2155